BOY'S EDITION

KIDS' MUSICAL THEATRE
AUDITION

INCLUDES A CD OF FULL PERFORMANCES & ACCOMPANIMENTS
COMPILED AND ARRANGED BY **MICHAEL DANSICKER**

ISBN-13: 978-1-4234-2880-0
ISBN-10: 1-4234-2880-3

HAL•LEONARD®
CORPORATION
7777 W. BLUEMOUND RD. P.O. BOX 13819 MILWAUKEE, WI 53213

T0056166

The following song is the property of:

Bourne Co.
Music Publishers
5 West 37th Street
New York, NY 10018

I'VE GOT NO STRINGS

Visit Hal Leonard Online at
www.halleonard.com

TABLE OF CONTENTS

Singers on the CD:
Anthony Colangelo (tracks 2, 3), **Noah Galvin** (5, 6, 8), **Sky Jarrett** (1, 9),
Daniel Marconi (4, 7, 10)

Piano:
Lawrence Yurman

Piano and Vocal Tracks recorded at: P.P.I. Recording, Inc., New York City
Tracks Engineered by Chip M. Fabrizi
Piano and Vocal Tracks produced by Michael Dansicker

Daniel Marconi

Theatre Credits: A WONDERFUL LIFE and NEW VOICES at the Papermill Playhouse.

Sky Jarrett

Broadway Credits: HOW THE GRINCH STOLE CHRISTMAS!, A CHRISTMAS CAROL, THE WILL ROGERS FOLLIES (tour); PARSIFAL at the Metropolitan Opera in New York.

Anthony Colangelo

Broadway Credits: NINE (2003 revival as Guido), A CHRISTMAS CAROL (Tiny Tim). Television: BLUES CLUES.

Noah Galvin

Theatre Credits: LES MISÉRABLES (National Tour), ACE (at the Old Globe Theatre), and currently in Cirque de Soleil's WINTUK.

Lawrence Yurman

Musical Director: GREY GARDENS. He has played and conducted the Broadway Productions of THOROUGHLY MODERN MILLIE, SIDE SHOW, and LES MISÉRABLES; and the Off-Broadway TWENTY FINGERS, TWENTY TOES! He is an active coach and accompanist in New York City.

This collection of songs has been compiled and arranged specifically to provide interesting, performable material to be used in the audition situation. In addition to the musical challenges of each piece, there is a dramatic unity and specificity in each number that greatly complements the singing element. The accompaniments are supportive of the lyrical content but do not always double the vocal line. To deliver a polished audition, the young performer must spend rehearsal time with a vocal coach, pianist, or the included recorded accompaniments.

To comply with the time limitations of a professional audition, each number is to be performed as presented, without any internal repetition. The keys have been selected to show a full vocal range: Boys (unchanged voices) and Girls (belt and head voice.) And happily, teenagers (along with pre-teens) will find this material a very useful addition to their repertoire and a great deal of fun to perform.

While the music selected is from the world of traditional musical theatre, the adaptation and arrangements are presented with a contemporary sensibility. These arrangements have been carefully developed over an extended period of time and have been very successful in helping a number of young singing actors realize their performance goals. At the request of many casting directors and agents, I am making this material available to everyone for the first time.

Whether auditioning for the spring school musical or a professional Broadway show, you will be on the right track performing any of the included songs. And perhaps these editions will help provide an answer to that most frequently asked question: "What should I sing at my audition?"

Michael Dansicker
New York City
September, 2007

Michael Dansicker
Arranger, composer, music director, orchestrator, and pianist on more than 100 Broadway and Off-B'way productions: from ALL NIGHT STRUT ('77) to Bob Dylan's THE TIMES THEY ARE A-CHANGIN' ('06). In the world of concert dance he has worked with Jerome Robbins, Agnes DeMille, Twyla Tharp, Geoffrey Holder, ABT, and the Joffrey. FILM(vocal supervisor): ELF, MEET THE PARENTS, ANALYZE THAT and scored the dances for Paramount's BRAIN DONORS. He is currently arranging and scoring the international dance production: AMERICAN DANCE! ('08) directed by Kenny Ortega. In addition to the many vocal tracks he has produced for Hal Leonard Corporation, he has created THE AUDITION SUITE (with Martin Charnin) and THE 16-BAR THEATRE AUDITION (4 volumes).

BUTTON UP YOUR OVERCOAT

from *Follow Thru*

Words and Music by B.G. DeSylva,
Lew Brown and Ray Henderson
Arranged by Michael Dansicker

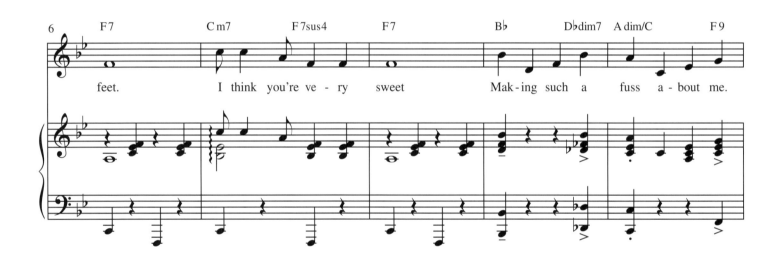

HALF THE BATTLE

from *Ben Franklin In Paris*

Lyrics by Sidney Michaels
Music by Mark Sandrich, Jr.
Arranged by Michael Dansicker

HIGH HOPES

from the Frank Capra film *A Hole in the Head*

Words by Sammy Cahn
Music by James Van Heusen
Arranged by Michael Dansicker

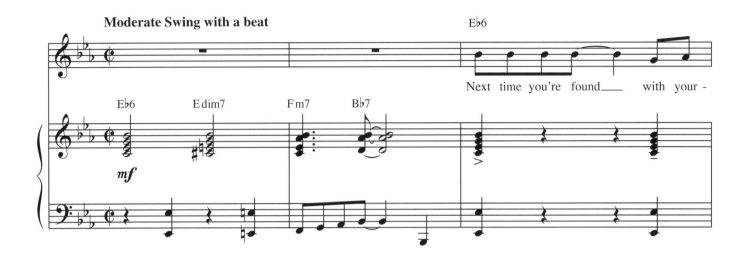

I'VE GOT NO STRINGS

from Walt Disney's *Pinocchio*

Words by Ned Washington
Music by Leigh Harline

JOIN THE CIRCUS

from *Barnum*

Music by Cy Coleman
Lyrics by Michael Stewart
Arranged by Michael Dansicker

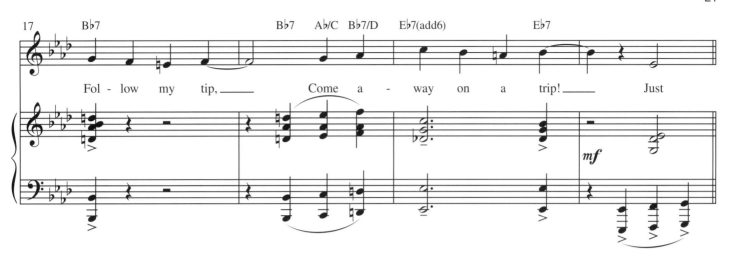

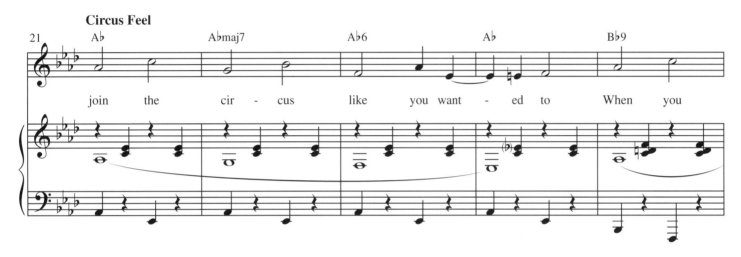

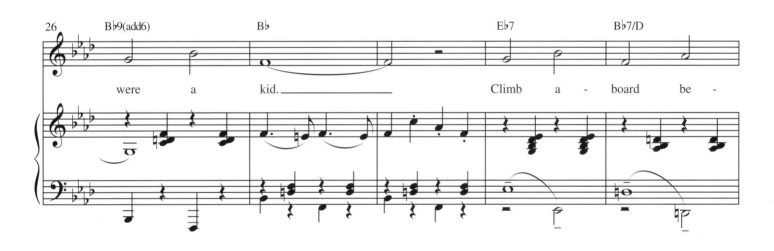

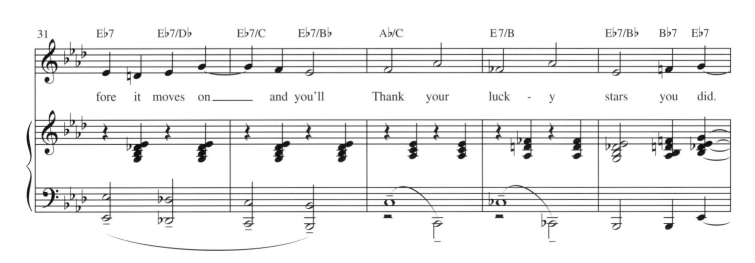

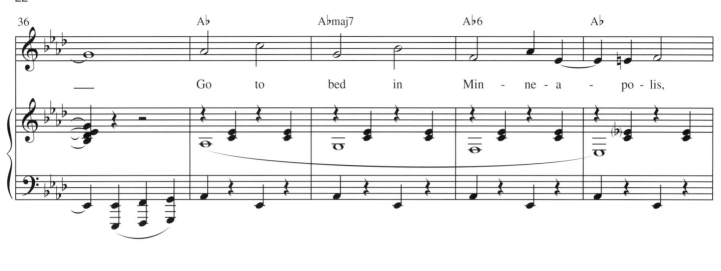

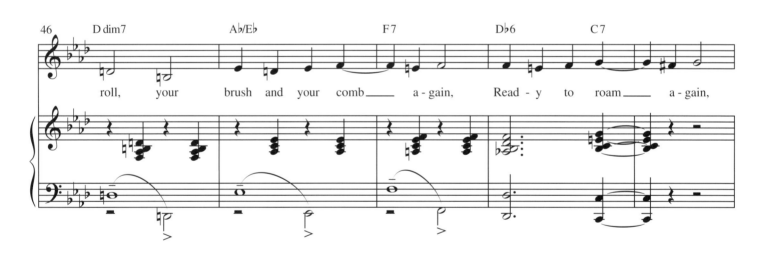

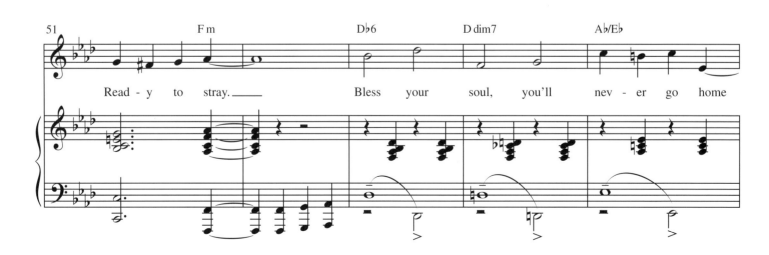

MY BABY JUST CARES FOR ME

from *Whoopee!*

Lyric by Gus Kahn
Music by Walter Donaldson
Arranged by Michael Dansicker

Broader, with a beat

MY BEST GIRL
from *Mame*

Music and Lyric by Jerry Herman
Arranged by Michael Dansicker

REAL LIVE GIRL

from *Little Me*

Music by Cy Coleman
Lyrics by Carolyn Leigh
Arranged by Michael Dansicker

SOMEBODY LOVES ME

from *George White's Scandals of 1924*

Words by B.G. DeSylva and Ballard MacDonald
Music by George Gershwin
Arranged by Michael Dansicker

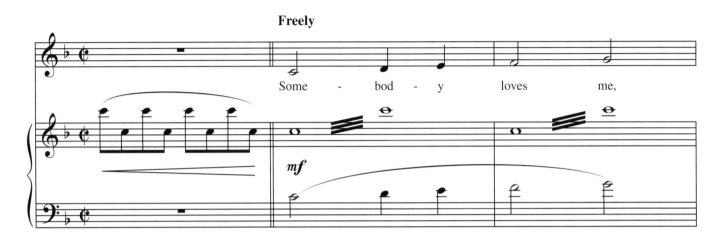

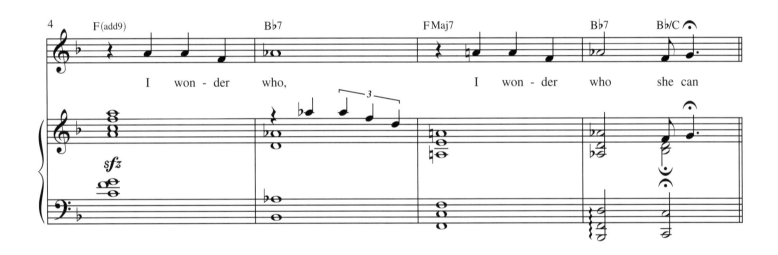

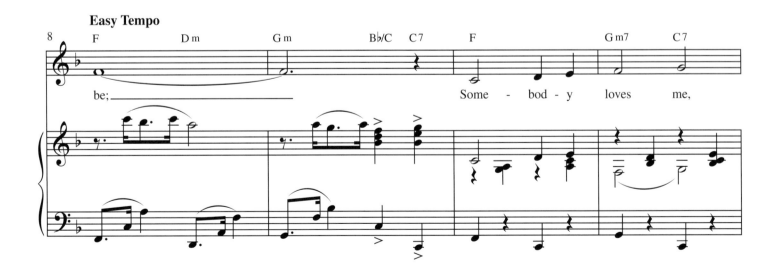

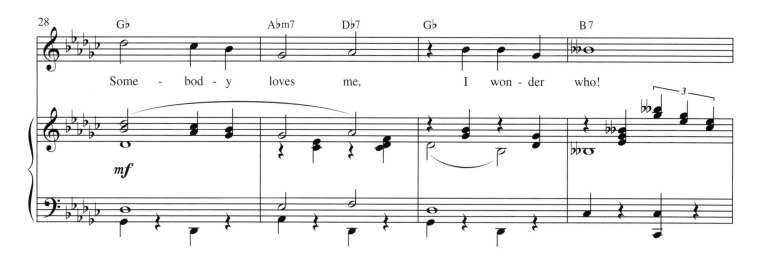

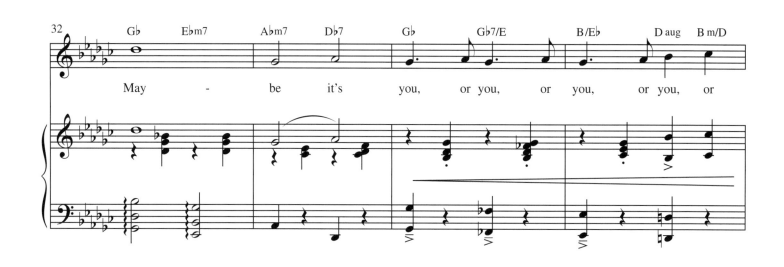

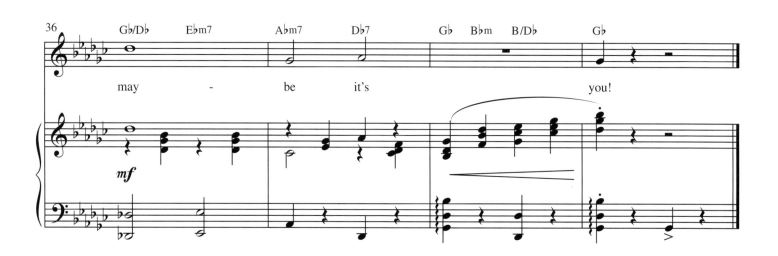

WHO DO YOU LOVE I HOPE

from *Annie Get Your Gun*

Music and Lyrics by Irving Berlin
Arranged by Michael Dansicker

ABOUT THE ENHANCED CD

In addition to piano accompaniments playable on both your CD player and computer, this enhanced CD also includes tempo adjustment and transposition software for computer use only. This software, known as Amazing Slow Downer, was originally created for use in pop music to allow singers and players the freedom to independently adjust both tempo and pitch elements. Because we believe there may be valuable educational use for these features in classical and theatre music, we have included this software as a tool for both the teacher and student. For quick and easy installation instructions of this software, please see below.

In recording a piano accompaniment we necessarily must choose one tempo. Our choice of tempo, phrasing, *ritardandos*, and dynamics is carefully considered. But by the nature of recording, it is only one option.

However, we encourage you to explore your own interpretive ideas, which may differ from our recordings. This new software feature allows you to adjust the tempo up and down without affecting the pitch. Likewise, Amazing Slow Downer allows you to shift pitch up and down without affecting the tempo. We recommend that these new tempo and pitch adjustment features be used with care and insight. Ideally, you will be using these recorded accompaniments and Amazing Slow Downer for practice only.

The audio quality may be somewhat compromised when played through the Amazing Slow Downer. This compromise in quality will not be a factor in playing the CD audio track on a normal CD player or through another audio computer program.

INSTALLATION INSTRUCTIONS:

For Macintosh OS 8, 9 and X:
- Load the CD-ROM into your CD-ROM Drive on your computer.
- Each computer is set up a little differently. Your computer may automatically open the audio CD portion of this enhanced CD and begin to play it.
- To access the CD-ROM features, double-click on the data portion of the CD-ROM (which will have the Hal Leonard icon in red and be named as the book).
- Double-click on the "Amazing OS 8 (9 or X)" folder.
- Double-click "Amazing Slow Downer"/"Amazing X PA" to run the software from the CD-ROM, or copy this file to your hard disk and run it from there.
- Follow the instructions on-screen to get started. The Amazing Slow Downer should display tempo, pitch and mix bars. Click to select your track and adjust pitch or tempo by sliding the appropriate bar to the left or to the right.

For Windows:
- Load the CD-ROM into your CD-ROM Drive on your computer.
- Each computer is set up a little differently. Your computer may automatically open the audio CD portion of this enhanced CD and begin to play it.
- To access the CD-ROM features, click on My Computer then right click on the Drive that you placed the CD in. Click Open. You should then see a folder named "Amazing Slow Downer". Click to open the "Amazing Slow Downer" folder.
- Double-click "setup.exe" to install the software from the CD-ROM to your hard disk. Follow the on-screen instructions to complete installation.
- Go to "Start," "Programs" and find the "Amazing Slow Downer" folder. Go to that folder and select the "Amazing Slow Downer" software.
- Follow the instructions on-screen to get started. The Amazing Slow Downer should display tempo, pitch and mix bars. Click to select your track and adjust pitch or tempo by sliding the appropriate bar to the left or to the right.
- Note: On Windows NT, 2000 and XP, the user should be logged in as the "Administrator" to guarantee access to the CD-ROM drive. Please see the help file for further information.

MINIMUM SYSTEM REQUIREMENTS:

For Macintosh:
Power Macintosh; Mac OS 8.5 or higher; 4 MB Application RAM; 8x Multi-Session CD-ROM drive

For Windows:
Pentium, Celeron or equivalent processor; Windows 95, 98, ME, NT, 2000, XP; 4 MB Application RAM; 8x Multi-Session CD-ROM drive